The Music We Make

By Clem King

Do you like music?

We could make some great music!

What different types of music shall we make?

Rolo taps out some music on this instrument.

He does soft taps over the top of the instrument.

He can do it solo.

Venus takes music lessons.

She pats out a basic beat on a drum.

Go, Venus!

Bo is a pupil
in a music program.

He can blow his sax
to make music!

At the moment,
he plays his sax solo,
but he wants
to join a band.

Eli's grandad is the best
at playing the banjo.

He is so great!
He even plays music
at the local bistro.

Eli's grandad

Eli wants to play
the banjo, too.

He can get a tip or two
from Grandad.
He and Grandad can begin
lessons today!

You can be a solo act
or you can be in a band.

I'm in a band with my siblings
Sam, Mabel and Flo.

I play the banjo in my band.

So, shall we make some crazy music?

CHECKING FOR MEANING

1. What instrument does Venus play? *(Literal)*
2. Is Bo in a band? *(Literal)*
3. Why would Grandad be a good banjo teacher for Eli? *(Inferential)*
4. Would you prefer to play music solo or in a band? Why? *(Evaluative)*

EXTENDING VOCABULARY

basic	Which vowel sound in the word *basic* is long and which one is short? What is the opposite of *basic*?
pupil	Is the letter *u* in the word *pupil* long or short? What is another word the author could have used instead of *pupil*?
bistro	What is a bistro? What is another word the author could have used instead of *bistro*?

MOVING BEYOND THE TEXT

1. What are some other instruments that you might hear in a band?
2. Which instrument would you most like to learn to play? Why?
3. What is your favourite kind of music?
4. A person who plays music is called a musician. How can a person become a good musician?

TIME TO WRITE

Write about your favourite song. What is it about? How does it make you feel?